The Ministry Of The Apostle

Thaddeus

J. P. Mendum

Kessinger Publishing's Rare Reprints

Thousands of Scarce and Hard-to-Find Books on These and other Subjects!

- Americana
- Ancient Mysteries
- Animals
- Anthropology
- Architecture
- Arts
- Astrology
- Bibliographies
- Biographies & Memoirs
- Body, Mind & Spirit
- Business & Investing
- Children & Young Adult
- Collectibles
- Comparative Religions
- Crafts & Hobbies
- Earth Sciences
- Education
- Ephemera
- Fiction
- Folklore
- Geography
- Health & Diet
- History
- Hobbies & Leisure
- Humor
- Illustrated Books
- Language & Culture
- Law
- Life Sciences
- Literature
- Medicine & Pharmacy
- Metaphysical
- Music
- Mystery & Crime
- Mythology
- Natural History
- Outdoor & Nature
- Philosophy
- Poetry
- Political Science
- Science
- Psychiatry & Psychology
- Reference
- Religion & Spiritualism
- Rhetoric
- Sacred Books
- Science Fiction
- Science & Technology
- Self-Help
- Social Sciences
- Symbolism
- Theatre & Drama
- Theology
- Travel & Explorations
- War & Military
- Women
- Yoga
- *Plus Much More!*

We kindly invite you to view our catalog list at:
http://www.kessinger.net

But further and stronger reasons for discrediting the story in every particular, will appear as we proceed to give a compendium of the other Syriac documents procured from the same source as this one, and in fact intimately connected therewith.

———◆———

CHAPTER XXXIII.

MINISTRY OF THE APOSTLE THADDEUS.

THE story of King Abgar and Jesus Christ, as given by Eusebius, breaks off at a point where Thaddeus declines to take the King's money. A mutilated Syriac document continues the narrative a little further. The first part of the story is missing in this manuscript, but what we have of it agrees so literally with the version of Eusebius that if it be not, as Dr. Cureton claims, "the original Aramaic document which Eusebius cites," it is at all events an early copy of the same story. It has a few variations from Eusebius's version, and consists of a single leaf, making only two printed pages in English; but fortunately the remainder of the story is supplied from another Syriac manuscript procured by the Abbot Moses at Bagdad in the year 931, which appears to be of the 6th century. Both these documents have Addeus instead of Thaddeus. Resuming the narrative at a point near the end of what has been already given, it reads as follows:

"And Abgar commanded them to give Addeus silver and gold. Addeus said to him, 'How can we receive that which is not ours? For lo! that which was ours have we forsaken, as we were commanded by our Lord; because without purses and without scrips, bearing the cross upon our shoulders, were we commanded to preach his Gospel in the whole creation, of whose crucifixion, which was for our sakes, for the redemption of all men, the whole creation was sensible and suffered pain.'"

Eusebius has given us only a sentence or two of the above, prefaced by another sentence not found in our document, to wit: "Abgar therefore commanded that in the morning all the people of his city should assemble and hear the preaching of Thaddeus." But this is manifestly only a bare statement of what follows. Thaddeus delivers a long discourse before the royal family, the court, and the people of the town, which is pretty fully reported to us by the King's scribe, as is attested at the end of the story, though it reads like the work of a priest of the 3d century. After relating the signs, wonders, and ascension, all details of which the reporter omits, Thaddeus tells them that Christ is coming again, when a general resurrection will take place and the righteous will be separated from the wicked, the sheep from the goats, the few from the many. Speaking of the crucifixion, he says:

"For though ye were not present at the time of Christ's suffering, yet from the sun which was darkened and which ye saw, learn ye and understand concerning the great convulsion which took place at that time, when he was crucified whose Gospel has winged its way through all the earth by the signs which his disciples, my fellows, do in all the earth. Yea, those who were Hebrews and knew only the language of the Hebrews, in which they were born, lo! at this day are speaking in all languages, in order that those who are afar off may hear and believe, even as those who are near. For he it is thåt confounded the tongues of the presumptuous in this region who were before us [Babel;] and he it is that teaches at this day the faith of truth and verity by us, humble and despicable men of Galilee and Palestine. For I also whom ye see am from Paneas [Cæsarea Paneas, now Baneas,] from the place where the river Jordan issues forth, and I was chosen together with my fellows to be a preacher."

This discourse is delivered immediately after the arrival of Thaddeus at Edessa, A. D. 29, according to the date given and accepted by Orthodox authority. It could not have been more than a year at most after the alleged crucifixion; and yet in that short interval we are here told that by the preaching of a few disciples the "Gospel has winged its way through all the earth." Edessa was at this time outside of the Roman Empire, whose domain extended 3,000 miles east and west by 1,500 north and south. Must we not suppose that these fellows were endowed not only with a supernatural gift of tongues, but with a miraculous mode of locomotion?

Passing over a considerable portion of the sermon, we come to this sentence:

"For lo! some even of the children of the crucifiers are become at this day preachers and evangelists with my fellow Apostles, in all the land of Palestine, and among the Samaritans, and in all the country of the Philistines; the idols also of Paganism are despised, and the cross of Christ is honored, and all nations and creatures confess God who became man."

Here certainly is a screw loose in the chronology. In the year of our Lord 29 "the *children* of the crucifiers are become preachers and evangelists, ... and *all nations and creatures* confess God who became man!"

Thaddeus then exhorts his hearers to believe the Gospel of Christ, so that the promise which Christ sent to them may be fulfilled, to wit:

"Blessed are ye that have believed in me, not having seen me; *and because ye have so believed in me the town in which ye dwell shall be blessed, and the enemy shall not prevail against it forever.*"

Here is an embarrassing point for the believers in the authenticity of this story. Thaddeus, in attempting to quote from the letter of Jesus to Abgar, interpolates what is indicated above in italics. Dr. Cureton tries to explain the discrepancy by supposing that the words are "either a message brought by Thaddeus himself, or much more probably a later interpolation; earlier however than

Ephraem Syrus, who alludes to them in his Testament."
ANTICHRIST has an easier solution of the difficulty, namely,
that the whole story is a fabrication of the 2d or 3d century, as all the circumstances tend to prove. If Ephraem
Syrus of the 4th century knew of a version containing
the above italicised words, how singular it is that in the
two versions that have come down to us, (one through
Moses of Chorene, 5th century,) and which agree most
literally, there is no such clause! Only think of the Son
of God bribing the people of Edessa to believe on him,
by promising to save their town forever from destruction
by the enemy!

At the close of his discourse Thaddeus says, "Let
those who have accepted the word of Christ remain with
us, and those also who are willing to join with us in
prayer." Public prayer has been a vital and indispensa-
ble element of all religious systems except that instituted
by Christ. He enjoined only secret prayer, and rebuked
those who prayed at the corners of the streets and in the
synagogues. How could Thaddeus have dared to con-
travene the express injunctions of his Lord? Nay, more,
with what audacity have the priesthood in all ages made
public prayer a paramount Christian duty, when Christ
himself never once prayed in public, but on the contrary
denounced those who do it as hypocrites!

Such was the effect of Thaddeus's discourse that " all
the city rejoiced in his teaching, men and women alike,
saying to him, ' True and faithful is Christ who sent thee
to us;'" and the King, Queen, and their two sons, Maanu
and Augustin, were numbered among the converts. Dr.
Cureton in a note here says that Abgar had two sons of
the name of Maanu, and this one, probably, was the elder
who succeeded his father at Edessa and reigned seven
years. But Moses of Chorene, an Armenian author of the

5th century, in his "History of Armenia," says that "after the death of Abgar the kingdom of Armenia was divided between two: Ananoun, Abgar's son, reigned at Edessa, and his sister's son, Sanadroug, in Armenia." (Ch. xxxiv.)

The King now told Thaddeus to proceed and build a church, saying that he was "prepared to give large donations" in order that those engaged in the work of the Lord "might not have any other work beside the ministry." He promised to honor Thaddeus's drafts for building purposes "without restriction," and to allow him to come, as one in authority, alone into the presence of his royal Majesty. A church was accordingly built, and in it were offered "vows and oblations."

Being asked by two of the chief men and rulers how Christ, being God, appeared to his disciples as a man, and how they were able to look upon him, Thaddeus "proceeded to satisfy them all about this," but in what way he satisfied them we are not told, except that he repeated before them "everything that the prophets had spoken concerning him." That is about all that the earliest writers tell us concerning a historical Christ, and is all we are permitted to know.

"But neither did King Abgar, nor yet the Apostle Addeus, compel any man by force to believe in Christ, because without the force of man the force of the signs compelled many to believe in him."

What lamb-like gentleness! Only signs and wonders were required in Apostolic times to compel belief; but when in after times signs and wonders failed, royal and papal edicts, with a realizing sense of a power behind the throne, seemed to be the only effectual means of saving souls.

Thaddeus employed a number of clerical assistants, four of whose names are given. One was Aggeus, a manufacturer of silk head-bands. One of the duties of these associate pastors, we are told, was "to read in the Old Testament and the New, and in the Prophets, and in the Acts of the Apostles." Here is an anachronism which Dr. Cureton tries to rectify by saying that as no other part of the New Testament was in existence at this time than the Hebrew Gospel of Matthew, this is probably what is meant. Yea, verily! the Gospel of Matthew in Hebrew read for the edification of Pagan converts in Mesopotamia! Thaddeus died, as Dr. Cureton thinks, about A. D. 40, and the earliest date now claimed for the writing of Matthew's Gospel is A. D. 64. Nevertheless, that or some other part of the New Testament is said to have been in use at Edessa between the years 29 and 40! Perhaps Thaddeus sent to Judea and elsewhere and obtained from Matthew, Mark, and Luke advance sheets of their Gospels, but as the book of Acts was not completed till about A. D. 64, when the events therein narrated terminate, Thaddeus must have had to content himself with only a fragment of the first part of that book.

In view of these difficulties, Dr. Cureton suggests that "the compiler of this account wrote some years subsequently to the events which he relates, or that it has been added by a later interpolator." But at the close of the document the writer's name is given as Labubna, the King's scribe, who says that according to the custom which existed in the kingdom, and by command of King Abgar himself, he committed these things to writing and deposited the same, attested by the seal of the proper officer, among the records of the kings.

But a still worse anachronism presently appears in the statement that these priests read not only from the Old Testament but from "the New of the Diatessaron." Dr. Cureton is not quite certain, but thinks the word is Diatessaron, referring to a work "which Tatian, the Syrian, compiled from the four Gospels (?) about the middle of the 2d century." (Between A. D. 170 and 180. Sup. Rel.) "If this be so," says Dr. C., "we have here a later interpolation." Yes, call it all a late interpolation, and you will probably be nearest the truth.

The mention of the observance of "the festivals of the church in their seasons," and of "the vigils every day," is incompatible with a system founded on the teachings of Christ within the first decade after his death. Nor is it credible that people from Assyria, "in the guise of merchants," became disciples, and received from Thaddeus "ordination to the priesthood," and on their return to their own country "erected houses of prayer there in secret, by reason of the danger from those who worshipped fire and paid reverence to water."

But now comes a still more incredible statement:

"Moreover, Narses, the King of the Assyrians, when he heard of those same things which Addeus the Apostle had done, sent a message to Abgar the King: 'Either despatch to me the man who doeth these things before thee, that I may see him and hear his word, or send me an account of all that thou hast seen him do in thy own town.' And Abgar wrote to Narses, and related to him the whole story of the deeds of Addeus from the beginning to the end, and he left nothing which he did not write to him. And when Narses heard those things which were written to him, he was astonished and amazed."

It so happens that Moses of Chorene has transmitted to us what purports to be a copy of the aforesaid letter to the Assyrian King at Babylon, and this is all it contains about "the whole story of Addeus," or anything pertaining thereto:

"But as to what you write to me about sending you the physician who works miracles and preaches another God superior to fire and water, that you may see and hear him, I say to you: he is not a physician according to the art of men; he is a disciple of the Son of God, Creator of fire and water; he has been appointed and sent to the countries of Armenia. ' But one of his principal companions, named Simon, is sent into the countries of Persia. Seek for him and you will hear him, you as well as your father Ardaches. He will heal all your diseases and will show you the way of life."

Great heavens! Behold Simon Kepha, *alias* Peter, away off in Persia before A. D. 40. He has travelled from Judea through Syria, Mesopotamia, Assyria, and Media into Persia, a journey of more than fifteen hundred miles, and there the Babylonian King is told to seek for him. Perhaps he did seek and find him, and thus by royal favor Simon established a church at Babylon, from whence the first Epistle of Peter, or rather Shemeun Kepha, was written. (1 Pet., v, 13.) This, after all, may be something more than a bald fiction, for another letter from Abgar to the King of Persia is given by Moses of Chorene, in which the statement is repeated that "Simon is in his Majesty's territories." For even if these letters are a forgery of the 2d or 3d century, there is no evidence of the existence of the first Epistle of Peter prior to the middle of the 2d century; and whenever it may have been written, it is far more likely that the salutation at the close from "the church at Babylon," means Babylon on the Euphrates, than the mystic Babylon on the Tiber, as the churchmen strive to interpret it.

Returning to our story, the next thing we find is, that Abgar, not being permitted to pass over Roman territory to punish the Jews for killing Christ, wrote a letter to Tiberius Cæsar. As we have two copies of the letter, let us place them side by side and see how they agree. The first version is by King Abgar's scribe, and the second by Moses, a historian of the 5th century. In order to make plain the discrepancies, we have italicised the more important parts in each one not contained in the other:

"King Abgar to our Lord Tiberius *Cæsar:* Although I know that nothing is hidden from thy Majesty, I write to inform *thy dread and mighty sovereignty* that the Jews who *are under thy dominion and* dwell in the country of Palestine have assembled themselves together and crucified *Christ* without any fault worthy of death, after he had done before them signs and wonders, and had shown them powerful mighty-works, so that he even raised the dead to life for them; and at the time they crucified him the sun became darkened and the earth also quaked, *and all created things trembled and quaked, and, as if of themselves, at this deed the whole creation and the inhabitants of the creation shrank away.* And now thy Majesty knoweth what is meet for thee to command concerning the people of the Jews who have done these things."

"Abgar, King *of Armenia,* to my Lord Tiberius, *Emperor of the Romans, greeting:* I know that nothing is unknown to your Majesty, but as your friend, I would make you better acquainted with the facts by writing. The Jews who dwell in the cantons of Palestine have crucified *Jesus: Jesus* without sin, *Jesus after so many acts of kindness,* so many wonders and miracles wrought for their good, even to the raising of the dead. *Be assured that these are not the effects of the power of a simple mortal, but of God.* During the time that they were crucifying him the sun was darkened, the earth was moved, shaken; *Jesus himself, three days afterwards, rose from the dead and appeared to many. Now, everywhere his name alone, invoked by his disciples, produces the greatest miracles: what has happened to myself is the most evident proof of it.* Your august Majesty knows henceforth what ought to be done in future with respect to the Jewish nation, which has committed this crime. *Your Majesty knows whether a command should not be published through the whole universe to worship Christ as the true God. Safety and health.*"

The word Christ, which occurs but once in the first version, is changed to Jesus in the second, where it is repeated three times in quick succession. The trembling and shrinking away of all creation and its inhabitants is omitted in the second version. The latter version interpolates an argumentative assurance that Jesus must have been God. Then it interpolates a statement about the resurrection of Jesus after three days, and his appearance to many. Also a statement that the bare invocation of his name by his disciples produces the greatest miracles, and an appeal to Abgar's own case as an illustration. And finally it has a suggestion to Tiberius to compel by royal command the worship of Christ as the true God.

But still worse discrepancies appear in the two versions of the answer of Tiberius :

"The letter of thy Fidelity towards me I have received, and it hath been read before me. Concerning what the Jews have dared to do in the matter of the cross, Pilate *the governor* also has written and informed *Aulbinus, my proconsul,* concerning these self-same things of which thou hast written to me. But, because a war with the people of Spain, who have rebelled against me, is on foot at this time, on this account I have not been able to avenge this matter ; but I am prepared, when I shall have leisure, to issue a command according to law against the Jews, who act not according to law. *And on this account as regards Pilate also, who was appointed by me governor there, I have sent another in his stead and dismissed him in disgrace, because he departed from the law and did the will of the Jews, and for the gratification of* the Jews crucified *Christ,* who, according to what I hear concerning him, instead of suffering the cross of death, deserved to be honored and worshipped by them : *and more especially because with their own eyes they saw everything that he did. Yet thou, in accordance with thy fidelity towards me, and the faithful covenant entered into by thyself and by thy fathers, hast done well in writing to me thus.*"

"Your kind letter has been read to me, *and I wish that thanks should be given to you from me. Though we had already heard several persons relate these facts,* Pilate has officially informed us of the miracles *of Jesus. He certified to us that after his resurrection from the dead he was acknowledged by many to be God. Therefore I myself also wished to do what you propose, but as it is the custom of the Romans not to admit a god merely by the command of the sovereign, but only when the admission has been discussed and examined in full Senate, I proposed the affair to the Senate, and they rejected it with contempt, doubtless because it had not been considered by them first. But we have commanded all those whom Jesus suits, to receive him amongst the gods. We have threatened with death any one who shall speak evil of the Christians.* As to the Jewish nation which has dared to crucify *Jesus,* who, as I hear, far from deserving the cross and death, was worthy of honor, worthy of the adoration of men, when I am free from the war with rebellious Spain, I will examine into the matter and will treat the Jews as they deserve."

How little of the two versions coincides ! As in the former case, the first of these has Christ once, while the second has Jesus three times. The important statement in the first version that Pilate had been dismissed in disgrace for ordering the crucifixion is not contained in the second. On the other hand, the second version contains the following new statements: 1. That after the resurrection of Jesus he was acknowledged by many to be God. 2. That Tiberius himself also wished to do what Abgar had suggested, namely, command the worship of Jesus as a God, and had even submitted the proposition to the Senate, but they had rejected it with contempt because it did not originate with them. 3. That Tiberius had nevertheless commanded believers in Jesus to receive him amongst the Gods, (a brilliant idea—like commanding water to run down hill!) and had threatened with death any one who should speak evil of the Christians!

We read in Acts that the disciples were first called Christians at Antioch about A. D. 43; but here is a letter in which the word is used, purporting to have been written by the Emperor Tiberius, who died A. D. 37. And as the circumstances show that it was not many months prior to the Emperor's death, the news of the crucifixion contained in the letter must have been about eight years old!

In the first version Albinus is mentioned as proconsul. Not till A. D. 62, in the reign of Nero, was there a Governor of Judea named Albinus. In another of these Syriac documents, the " Exit of Mary," it is stated that Sabina (Sabinus) was procurator under Tiberius, with jurisdiction as far as the Euphrates. But that is not true. Vitellius was Governor of Syria between A. D. 35 and 39, and removed Pilate from the administration of Judea; therefore Dr. Cureton says that the person named as Albinus can only be Vitellius! Hear! Hear!

But how about the war with Spain spoken of in both versions? No mention of such a war is made by any his-

torian. So Dr. Cureton gets over the difficulty by supposing that as "Vitellius about this time was mixed up
with the wars of the Parthians and Hiberians, and as
Hiberi is a name common to Spaniards as well as Hiberians, the apparent error may have arisen in translating the
letter out of Latin into Syriac." But the same error
must also have been made by the Armenian scribe in the
other version. Moreover the people of Hiberi, or Iberi,
on the Caspian sea, were at this time beyond the Roman
jurisdiction; how, then, could they "rebel" against
Tiberius?

This letter from Tiberius is said to have been sent by
one Aristides; who returned with suitable presents to the
Emperor from Abgar. In returning he is said to have
stopped at Thicuntha, an unknown place, and to have
reached Tiberius at Artica. This, Dr. Cureton thinks,
may be intended for Ortygia, near Syracuse, which he
says was not far from the Island of Capreæ, where Tiberius then resided. Then Aristides related before Tiberius
the mighty works which Thaddeus had done. "And
when Tiberius had leisure from the war, he sent and put
to death some of the chief men of the Jews in Palestine,"
for which merited punishment King Abgar "rejoiced
greatly."

All this journey of Aristides to Edessa and back was
begun and ended before Pilate, who had been recalled,
was able to reach Rome; for when he got there Tiberius
was dead. In other words, Aristides travelled at least
three times as fast as Pilate did, whose recall would seem
to have required him to make haste home, while the former, being charged with the delivery of an answer to a
letter that seemed to have been seven or eight years in
coming, could have appropriately adopted the motto of

the preceding Emperor Augustus, *Festina lente*—"make haste slowly."

Such was the progress of the Gospel at Edessa that churches were soon built in the adjacent villages and administered by deacons and elders. But in due course of time Thaddeus, being taken sick and about to die, appointed Aggeus, the manufacturer of royal head-bands, Guide and Ruler in his stead. The title of Bishop (*episcopos*) had not yet obtained in that region. Thaddeus in his last hours especially enjoined upon his people to "have no fellowship with the Jews, the crucifiers." But the Jews of Edessa must have cherished a more tolerant spirit, for it is said that his death was bitterly mourned not only by the Christians, (here again this word occurs about A. D. 40,) but by the Jews also. No one lamented the Apostle's death more than Abgar, who showed his grief by ordering a grand funeral, and Thaddeus, who "possessed not anything in this world," was "buried like one of the princes, with great and surpassing pomp, in a grand sepulchre adorned with sculpture."

Aggeus, like his priestly predecessor, refused all gifts; "instead of receiving gold and silver, he himself enriched the church of Christ with the souls of believers." The church-members, both male and female, "lived like anchorites," and their conduct was so chaste and holy that "even the [Pagan] priests of the house of Nebu and Bel divided the honor with them at all times." That is, the Christians adapted their new religion to the times, and affiliated with the worshippers of many gods; because, in spite of the previous allegation that Christianity had become the State religion and was embraced by all the people, it seems that all the while there were priests of Nebu and Bel who "divided the honor" with the priests of Christ.

King Abgar did not long survive his Apostolic pastor. He died, says Dr. Cureton, A. D. 45, and as the ministry of Thaddeus is supposed by Dr. C. to have lasted about ten or eleven years, the Apostle must have died five or six years before the King—*i. e.*, about A. D. 40, as heretofore stated.   Abgar was succeeded by one of his sons, but which one or what his name was we are left in doubt. Moses of Chorene says it was Ananoun, but Dr. Cureton says it must have been Maanu—that Abgar had two sons of that name, and that "the elder probably succeeded his father at Edessa and reigned seven years."   Our document names two sons, Maanu and Augustin, and now near the close of it we read as follows:

"And some years after the death of Abgar the King, there arose one of his contumacious sons, who was not favorable to peace; and he sent word to Aggeus as he was sitting in the church: 'Make me a head-band of gold, such as thou usedst to make for my fathers in former times.'   And Aggeus sent word to him: 'I will not give up the ministry of Christ which was committed to me by the disciple of Christ, and make a head-band of wickedness.'   And when he saw that he did not comply, he sent and brake his legs as he was sitting in the church expounding.   And as he was dying he adjured Palut and Abshelama: 'In this house, for whose truth's sake, lo! I am dying, lay me and bury me.'   And even as he had adjured them, so did they lay him—inside the middle door of the church, between the men and the women.   And there was great and bitter mourning in all the church, and in all the city—over and above the anguish and the mourning which there had been within the church, such as had been the mourning when Addeus the Apostle himself died."

Dr. Cureton thinks the contumacious royal priest-killer was the second son Maanu, whose reign began about A. D. 52.   Anyhow, he was a pretty hard Christian.

But now comes the close of the narrative, which caps the climax of anachronism, as will be seen by the dates in parentheses:

" And in consequence of his dying suddenly and quickly at the breaking of his legs, he was not able to lay his hand upon Palut. So Palut went to Antioch and received ordination to the priesthood from Serapion, Bishop of Antioch, (about A. D. 189;) by which Serapion himself also ordination had been received from Zephyrinus, Bishop of the city of Rome, (A. D. 202–219,) in the succession of the ordination to the priesthood from Simon Cephas, [Kipha, *alias* Petros,] who had received it from our Lord, and was Bishop there in Rome twenty-five years in the days of the Cæsar, [Claudius] who reigned there thirteen years, (A. D. 41–54.)"

Dr. Cureton has to give up this part entirely. He says it is "a barefaced interpolation made by some ignorant person much later." Very likely; but is not the whole story a fabrication of the 2d or 3d century? To us there is nothing in it to command belief, but many things that stamp it as a baseless fiction, and we are amazed at the credulity of a scholar who accepts any essential part of the story as fact. The translator of our document, the Rev. B. P. Pratten, in his preface admits that doubt is cast upon the conversion of Abgar the black, by the statement in Bayer's History of Edessa that Abgar Bar Manu, who reigned between A. D. 160 and 170, is the first King of Edessa on whose coins symbols of the Baal-worship of the country are wanting, these being replaced in his case by the sign of the cross. This evidence the translator admits to be very strong if it refers to a complete series of the coins of Edessa. But he thinks there is proof at all events in other Syriac documents that Christianity was introduced into Mesopotamia early in the 2d century. These documents we will next consider. But we submit that we have adduced enough evidence to show that the story of Abgar and Jesus Christ, together with that of the Ministry of Thaddeus, is a clumsy fabrication.

Not with anger but with pity do we assail the belief in these legends. Ridicule and sarcasm are proper weapons to be used against credulity, but anger has no place in the bosom of reason.   The rationalist knows that belief is not a matter of volition, therefore he can repeat with pleasure the lines of Dr. Watts as hereby amended and adultified:

Let dogs delight to bark and bite,
    For 'tis their nature to;
Let angry bigots growl and fight,
    Their God hath made them so;
But men of sense will never let
    Vindictive passions rise;
The light within was never set
    To blind the mental eyes.

CHAPTER XXXIV.

THE CRUCIFIXION A. D. 29—THE ASCENSION AT PENTECOST.

THE same Syriac manuscript in which the story of the Ministry of Thaddeus is found, contains another entitled "Teaching of the Apostles."   It begins thus:

"At what time Christ was taken up to his Father; and how the Apostles received the gift of the spirit, and the ordinances and laws of the church; and whither each one of the Apostles went; and from whence the countries in the territories of the Romans received the ordination to the priesthood.

"In the year 339 of the kingdom of the Greeks, in the month Heziran, on the 4th day of the same, which is the first day of the week, and the end of Pentecost—on the self-same day came the disciples from Nazareth of Galilee, where the conception of our Lord was announced, to the mount which is called that of the Place of Olives, our Lord being with them, but not being visible to them. And at the time of early dawn our Lord lifted up his hands and laid them upon the heads of the eleven disciples, and gave them the gift of the priesthood.   And suddenly a bright cloud received him. And they saw him as he was going up to heaven."

This is the end of this publication.

Any remaining blank pages are for our book binding
requirements and are blank on purpose.

To search thousands of interesting publications like this one,
please remember to visit our website at:

http://www.kessinger.net

CPSIA information can be obtained
at www.ICGtesting.com
Printed in the USA
BVHW011741070920
588229BV00011B/1579